Creative Learning in the Local Church

Meg Orr

Researcher in Lay Learning

GROVE BOOKS LIMITED

RIDLEY HALL RD CAMBRIDGE CB3 9HU

Contents

Acknowledgments

First and foremost, I would like to offer my heartfelt thanks to the lay people of St Mary and St Cuthbert's Church, Chester-le-Street, in the Diocese of Durham. Had you not come along to my teaching sessions this booklet could never have been written. I am also grateful to Roly Riem, Alan Jeans and Judith Rossall for their guidance and insightful comments. I would also like to thank Jeff Astley for being my sounding board, John Pritchard for giving me the nudge I needed to finish the booklet and Alan Suggate for speaking good sense. And finally, my special thanks must go to my husband Geoff for his unfailing support.

The Cover Illustration is by Terry Culkin

First Impression August 2005

ISSN 0262-799X

ISBN 1 85174 600 5

Introduction 1

To talk only in terms of what theology is, rather than what theology can do, is to miss the mark.

This booklet is a celebration of lay people doing theology. It is a recognition of God with us, a God who engages directly with us. It celebrates acceptance, desire, risk, intimacy, longing and belonging. It also celebrates the preparation of our hearts and minds before God by doing a theology which is an integrated theology. This includes the life of prayer, our spirituality, our awareness for continual conversion and a sense of mission and purpose of who we are in the world. It is a celebration of love come down because we are a people in love—for we are loved by one who is love. In our desire to share that love, we taste it, and see it and feel it and own it for ever. We are partakers, co-creators with God. Because God loves, we love. Because God moves, we move. We are with God and only with God because God graciously gives of himself. God desires us. We desire God and so the embrace of God on our lives keeps us in perfect union with him. We are co-creators with God.

But is this, I wonder, fully understood by lay and clergy in parish life? Do we offer a co-creating integrated theology which captivates the heart and mind and makes sense of the here and now? Or do we have a private theology, a closed theology, unapproachable, intellectually stultifying and lacking intimacy?

Do we offer a co-creating integrated theology which captivates the heart and mind and makes sense of the here and now?

When I first began to use the word theology in my church I came in for some criticism from lay and clergy alike. 'Is it not for the middle classes?' 'Aren't you biting off more than you can chew?' 'Doesn't it smack of academia and intellectualism?' Well it can, I said, but it does not have to. Nevertheless, doing theology in the parish setting means taking risks and is not as straightforward as we think. I believe that we need to be more aware of some of the things that have been said about theology and ourselves. You

Doing theology in the parish setting means taking risks

may very well want to ask, when so much seems stacked against it, how our hearts and minds can be won over. Here are some examples:

- An eminent bishop speaking about theology and the laity said, 'Don't tell them what it is, just do it.'
- One theologian has written that, 'Many people see theology as something of a handicap complicating simple faith and piety, certainly not good for the punters and at best the curious interest of a few rarefied souls.'[1] This seems to be saying that whatever theology is, we are not going to get far with it, so do not bet your life on it. It bamboozles and attracts the odd.
- Another theologian recognizes that the laity are 'theologically out of sight, out of mind.'[2] When it comes to doing theology, lay people are not included. If this is so, then no wonder lay people have nothing to say. We have never really been given the opportunity to understand the nature of theology or why we should be doing it in the parishes. We believe it smacks of academia and therefore freezes our response, rendering many of us incoherent. It excludes. As a result we are unnerved by theology and have every right to feel out of it, although this is a sad admission. To be theologically out of sight out of mind is to be an onlooker or, worse still, invisible. We are not recognized *in* theology or *by* theology and therefore have no voice. We do not participate because we have not quite made it, have not quite got there. How I wish we could wave a magic wand but it is not as simple as that. I want to ask where *are* we in all of this?

I have been doing theology in my church for 20 years and what I try to offer in this booklet is a modest account of a way of doing it in a parish setting. It is risk laden, sometimes unnerving but at the same time rewarding. It is not a blow by blow account—more an attempt to capture a spiritual receptivity and a spiritual creativity which keeps us alive to God.

It is a temptation where we can boldly say, 'I can, Lord, try me!'

What I advocate is a theology of desire, a desire that sometimes makes us go weak at the knees in adoration. It is a journey towards God, incomplete in this life, with unexpected twists and turns and temptations, but desirous of indescribable things to come here, on earth, as in heaven. I am a great believer in God's temptation, because we worship a God who tempts us to learn of him, and to follow him in order to become like him. It is a temptation where we can boldly say, 'I can, Lord, try me!'

There is nothing grandiose here—we meet, clergy and laity, as fellow workers keeping faith with God, believing that he hears and speaks. We meet because life is a celebration of God's love and of God's desire for us. Only a redeemed people can feel the depth of this love. We meet because life is our loving and living desire for God. We meet because life is a life of learning and a call to obedience. Indeed, I believe that God's spirit of learning is caught up in the whole passion and desire of God because God and passion are the essentials for living. It is, I believe, deeply woven into our life's experiences, and not to acknowledge this is to dishonour God. If 'the glory of God is humans fully alive,' then we have to play our part. Our response to God's temptation, I believe, comes from a creative urge or desire which God plants in each of us. Doing theology is to be tempted by this urge, and is part of life's blood, something that we feel in our bones. Truly we are wonderfully made, but made for response to God.

Truly we are wonderfully made, but made for response to God

First Person

When I first started to write about doing theology in my church it took me some time before I could allow myself to write in the first person. It seemed bold, brash and rather egotistical. But over a period of time, as I grew more confident, it gradually dawned on me that there was no right or wrong way of writing. I write because I have something to say; it is normal and natural and from the heart. I suppose you could say I am writing my own authentic theology. It is my hope that those who read this booklet may feel encouraged to write their own theology not as a literary exercise but as a spiritual quest.

Of course, I am aware that there are opportunities up and down the country for lay people to study theology in more depth and for some this can be very rewarding. However my concern lies with the vast majority of church-goers who, for a variety of reasons, are unable to pursue a course of study and so remain largely untouched by an everyday theology which tries to make sense of faith and life.

When theology and education meet one sparks off the other and gives an energy and a sense of urgency to everything

I am also concerned about the role of the teacher in the church, the importance of the teacher as a person, and the value we place on education. I have found that when theology and education meet we have an explosive mix. One sparks off the other and gives an energy and a sense of urgency to everything.

Sometimes we make it very difficult for people to believe. Explaining doctrine, telling the truth, leaves little room for the use of creative imagination. Too many words inhibit and we drown or flounder. Teaching can be in danger of becoming dictatorial, weighing heavily upon the soul. There are times when I feel we need less catechesis and more imagination. Over the years I have come to learn that the *way* we learn something is more influential than the *something* we learn. I have found that the use of pictures, posters, prayers, poems as well as passages of Scripture help to stir the imagination when we do theology. And I have also come to learn that *where* we learn is equally important, because when anything is local, it is real. It is 'this place, just as it is, these people in their everyday clothes—we accept whoever happens to be on the premises as the people of God.'[3]

There are times when I feel we need less catechesis and more imagination

What I have written, I hope, will speak of a God who longs to be known, who longs to be found and who is unfailing love.

Falling in Love with Theology 2

I fell in love with theology when I was forty.

It was not sudden—more of a lingering swoon. I had been a rather reluctant, hesitant and sometimes unhappy sheep outside the fold, until I had the good fortune to attend a series of Bible study sessions taken by our Rector's wife. She was a gracious, gifted and patient teacher, who left the gate of the sheep-fold open long enough for me to step inside in my own time. It was a 'heady' experience; what had been in my bones for some years was now becoming part of my life blood. Truth had caught up with me, and I could not conceal my joy. A few months later I applied to my local university, and to my surprise was accepted as an undergraduate to read for a theology degree. The love affair was serious.

I recall an evening in a pub with a friend. He was about to start a new job and he asked me if I had any plans for the future. I told him I was going to study theology. He paused, looked at me and said, 'Was it the only thing available?' The scene moves to a hospital and a meeting with a consultant. As he flicked through my notes he saw that I did not work and asked me what I did to fill in my time. I told him of my interest in theology. He gave me a rather wan smile. Easing the needle out of my arm, he studied me and said, 'By the way, what *is* theology?' To round it off an old friend said, 'Well, it's only Scripture!' We laughed, but it did make me think. I had met with incredulity and naivety. Did I share these attitudes? Yes, because my theological journey was to take me, more often than not, into uncharted waters, and I did not enjoy being out of my depth.

My theological journey was to take me into uncharted waters, and I did not enjoy being out of my depth

Theology thrilled me and drilled me. I was surrounded by young high-fliers who were exhilarating, and how I envied them their energy. We soon realized that theology was not going to be handed to us on a platter; rather, the course was to teach us how to search and explore for meaning. As I pursued my studies I believe something other than academic theology was sustaining me in this demanding work which was to transform my life and my calling. Theology did not attract me because it tried to explain or justify itself, rather it was the way in which it lured and tempted and called me out. Is not this how God works? Its attraction was like that of a love affair. I was drawn, wooed. I could not help myself. I only knew I wanted to be in the presence of another. It was a fizzy, heady experience which brushed up against me and lingered. I was filled with new sensations and new horizons. I was caught up by a theology of desire, by its very spirit and life. My thinking was taken up into a way of being, with body, mind and soul integrated into one.

One theologian comes close to what I am trying to say, when he describes theology as 'a disposition of the soul towards God,'[4] something he says we have lost nowadays when we come to do theology. Is this 'disposition of the soul' a preparation of our hearts and minds before God? Is this an acknowledgment of all that we are and all we are meant to be? And are we drawn by the very dynamics of theology itself and the delights that it holds, so that when we participate in it, it becomes part of our inheritance, part of our life's blood, our *raison d'être* and our eternal hope? I believe it is and I believe we are all invited to share in it.

Theology, like the attentive lover, will not leave us alone. It persists in our restlessness. St Augustine sums up our longing when he says, 'God and man have but one desire: to meet!' They are tremendous words for he knows that when this meeting takes place we will want more. Our natural desires and our ultimate concerns will be released so that we are left to reflect freely upon our experiences of God. And so we find ourselves doing theology when we uncover the known and the unknown, when we meet with certainty and uncertainty as we move into the heart of God. It invites us to be in touch with the mystery of our own being and to enjoy that mystery. For some it simply gets curiouser and curiouser!

Theology for All

I do not believe theology to be an esoteric subject, intelligible only to select groups of people. Nor is it a psychological description of what our basic convictions happen to be. Theology claims to be concerned with what *ought* to be the basic convictions of everyone of us. When we come to use words, however indirectly, to indicate truth about God, then we have to discover the meaning behind these words so that faith is broadened and deepened. God is present to us all even when we have few ideas about him and yet this should not make us complacent, because theology gives us a voice. But more than that it spurs us into action and prepares us spiritually by giving us confidence so that we draw upon our natural desires, concerns and enterprises, and put them to use in imaginative ways

Theology helps us to understand mission in its broadest sense

in all sorts of settings and circumstances. This surely is a practical theology where everyone can take part and feel at home. This is also part and parcel of the mission of the church because theology helps us to understand mission in its broadest sense.

A theology of desire, the very spirit of theology, has the power to send us out 'to proclaim the good news of the kingdom, to teach and baptize and nurture new believers, to respond to human need by loving service, to seek to transform the unjust structures of society, to strive to safeguard the integrity of creation and sustain and renew life on earth.'[5] By being sent out, we can learn to be a holy, learning and witnessing people. I wanted to do theology with lay people so that we could lift up our hearts and go on asking if persistence in faith is justified despite doubts and despite hurts, and whether we would find something to celebrate. In short, is theology worth it? I hoped that whatever I taught would reflect these concerns and questions, so that they could become part of our life blood and an expression of our own identity.

By being sent out, we can learn to be a holy, learning and witnessing people

Putting Your Heart into Theology

There are some who may see this theology of desire as a rather cosy, sentimental and individualistic journey which is all heart. I know we can be an unbalanced sort of people in that our affections may run riot. But unless our hearts are in theology we will never feel its thrill. After the thrill comes the drill and the discipline when we are compelled to use a wider imagination so that we might discover and reflect more broadly. I believe we can all come to love and do theology this way.

One of the ways of coming alive and feeling inspired often depends on how we allow theology, like the Spirit, to settle upon us and work in us. I call this being at home, being at ease and being caught up by the 'spirit of theology.' It requires a lightness of touch which is nevertheless compelling, and it should be free to blow where it will—which makes it exciting. How does this spirit of theology work? It works by having the willingness to participate in and reflect upon belief in God so that we come to desire to speak coherently about our faith and all that we hold dear. In all of this we have to include the life of worship and prayer, for theology would be very sterile if something like this was not going on inside us. Our praise gives release to our souls so that we may come to know the awesome majesty of God and his salvation. Our prayer gives rise to prayers of meditation so that we can immerse ourselves in the truths of the Christian faith by allowing them to enter our very being.

Theology needs to be trusted with our hearts and minds so that we may know God and be known by him. Only by trusting in theology will it begin to work in us, because at the heart of theology is *encounter* which not only evokes *response* from the people of God but enriches all our strivings to *be* the people of God. To trust theology means to take a chance; it requires us to be imaginative and to recognize change. To trust theology means to be ready to explore and to respond.

We are all making theology simply through the process of living

I have met lay people and clergy who dismiss theology by saying that it just washes over people. Well yes, if we stop to think for a moment, that is exactly what it does. It is like life. It settles and seeps and soaks into us and makes us human. But I also meet lay people who want to give theology a go so that we come to learn that we are all making theology simply through the process of living. One of the big questions for the churches is how do we harness the theology inside us and what do we do with it?

Coming Together

I drew together a group of women, 16 in all, and we met for six afternoon sessions. As we introduced ourselves one lady, in her eighties, and who spoke with the thick Swiss accent of her origin said, 'I have come here today because you don't know what to believe zeez days!' Another lady in her seventies said, 'I have come here because I have a thirst for knowledge.' Music to my ears. It was time to go to the biblical text and I chose the wedding at Cana (John 2). But before we read it I asked them to walk down memory lane with me. What was your wedding day like? How did you look? Who was there? Weddings seem to bring families, relations and strangers together. It is all new. What did it feel like to be married? Did you have hopes and expectations? Have they come true? Have you coped with the ups and downs of married life? Where was God in all of this? What do our experiences tell us about God, ourselves and our place in the world?

It was at this point that some of the older ladies in the group shared something about their widowhood. They spoke of how they coped with the death of their husbands and how living alone was difficult. Some of the younger women spoke of motherhood and about their 'first born' and the specialness of it all. Here was an opportunity for these women, married and unmarried, 'to see the living God at work in womanly ways, a time to bring widowhood and experiences of marriage, child-bearing, menopause and ageing into Christian life and worship.'[6]

That Wedding! (Reflections from the group)

The excitement and expectation for this wedding in Cana was clearly felt, more so because we had all been invited! It was a glorious day and the bride looked radiant. The world and his wife were there and celebration and thanksgiving were in the air as the wine flowed freely. There was a lot of coming and going and apparently some consternation but it did not spoil the day.

One of the stewards: 'You'll never believe it! One minute water, the next minute wine! When Jesus asked me to draw water from the water pots some of it slopped on my hand. I hastily licked my hand dry and yes, you've guessed it, it was the sweetest wine I've ever tasted. You know I could have sworn that Jesus gave me a nod and a wink. I don't understand any of it. I just kept on pouring.'

Local drunk: 'What a wedding! Half way through there was a bit of a commotion.

Rumour had it that the wine was running out. Can you believe it! I could not see quite clearly (I'd had one or two), but a man called Jesus seemed to take charge and there was a bit of comin' and goin.' Suddenly it was all right and there were drinks all round again. Someone filled my cup 'til it was running over. Not that I'm complainin.' I know this, when there's another wedding in Cana, and if that man Jesus is invited, I'll be there!'

Mary, Mother of Jesus: 'I remember feeling a deep sense of urgency about my son. He was special. I cannot quite put it into words but something made me realize that my son was no ordinary man and must be obeyed. I have pondered these things in my heart and I don't fully understand. Water become wine? What's it all about?'

We picked up Mary's thoughts and her sense of urgency about her son. What was it about Jesus that made people respond? Why was everything so confusing and mysterious? Why all this new wine? What on earth is happening here? Did we blink and miss it? Mary's questions became our questions. But we also needed to ask what this miracle was saying about God, and ourselves and our place in the world. An extravagant God? An extravagant love! An over-the-top God? A generosity of spirit that is simply breathtaking. We are invited to drink of the new wine, to partake of the new life in Jesus, which is sparkling, rich, fresh, fruitful and liberating. Our lives are to be brimful with the generosity of a bounteous God.

These are just some of the things we reflected and pondered over as we tried to see and seek God's purpose in our lives. Whoever we are, and however we see ourselves, God sees more, because there is more for us. God values our achievements as single women, wives, widows and mothers, both in the home and in the work place. This is because we matter, and mattering matters. This is newness of life. For some of us this might mean picking up the courage to speak to someone about faith, or it may mean finding the strength through friendship to cope with the loneliness, loss, frailty and sickness in ourselves and in others. Perhaps some new insights may help us to think in positive ways about marriage and relationships and the awesome responsibility of raising children and keeping the family together. There again our worship and our work place may provide the opportunity for witness where we can bring before God the needs of the world, which can spur us into activity by quickening our sense of social injustice. Indeed worship, the work place and theology are soul mates because liturgy, like theology, allows us to speak, allows us to hear our own voice. The words, 'O Lord open our lips,' and the response, 'And our mouth shall show forth your praise,' liberate us to express how we feel about God, ourselves and the world. But this is not enough. All that we bring before God in worship needs to be heard and spoken about in the parishes. By doing theology in the local setting we make the attempt to reflect on what God is saying and doing with us here and now. By doing theology we are seeking, seeing, discovering, finding and reflecting on God in our lives and it brings out the best in us. Whoever we are and whatever we do, we are part of the mainstream of life, because we share in God's world.

By doing theology in the local setting we make the attempt to reflect on what God is saying and doing with us here and now

At the end of the afternoon session we tasted the new wine. One of the ladies in the group was dying. Her eyes met mine in a steady gaze as she raised her glass and said quietly, 'To life in Jesus.' She is now with her Lord living her new life.

3

Deeper and Broader

Reaching Out

How could I reach another cross section of people, bearing in mind that many led busy working lives and not all of them wanted a six to eight week course? I decided to hold a series of drop-into-theology teaching sessions. Each session was to be complete in itself but all of them had the theme of expectation and celebration. Personal invitations were handed out as well as a careful canvassing of the parish. To my surprise they were well attended, and whilst we were mainly women, there was a sprinkling of men. They make such a difference to the dynamics of a group when they are willing to take part. Here are some highlights of the drop-in sessions.

How could I reach another cross section of people, bearing in mind that many led busy working lives?

I began one session with some Jewish customs, and in particular with the Passover. As we read the Passover passages I wanted to capture the inner spirit of Judaism—the excitement and the hopes and dreams of the Jewish people. And so we asked the question, 'Why was Passover night so special?' Something momentous had happened. There was a Moses rescue, and an Exodus in haste.

As we read Passover passages I wanted to capture the inner spirit of Judaism

We chewed on unleavened bread, straw-like, dry, tasteless, unfinished and made in a hurry. Bondage killed the spirit and dulled the senses. We dipped our fingers into salt water and put them to our lips. The life of slavery had been bitter for the Hebrews; the saltiness lingered. We savoured sweet haroseth (nuts, fruit and honey), and the sweetness of freedom, reminding us that the Israelites were free to lead a new life. We sprawled in our chairs (as best we could), reclining at ease, without anxiety, as free men and women. How did the Jews see God? Unlike the Greeks who ruminated and philosophized on the nature of God, to the Jews, God *is!* He had spoken and acted and his words and deeds were there for all to see.

The Jews did not have a god, they had God. And so the Exodus of the Jewish people was God's great saving act in their history, when he made himself known by delivering them from bondage and taking them to the promised land.

I hoped that we might all go out, setting our face towards the challenges of life in the world, strengthened by our resolve

We drank of the Passover wine long and deep, and we raised our glasses and allowed something of that momentous occasion to soak into our own lives. There was much to reflect on here. When have our lives been dusty, dry, tasteless, bitter or sweet? What might God be saying to us? How can we be refreshed? When was the last time that God had done a new thing in our lives? It may not have been earth shattering, but were we able to read the signs? What may have prevented us from hearing God's call and his promise of new life? There were many stories to share either in the privacy of the small group or in the wider group. Were our conversations 'preparing our hearts before God?' Was our theology 'a disposition of the soul towards God?' Were we drawn by its delights and revelations? All I can say is that some of the experiences we shared with one another sounded very much to be part of our life blood and our *raison d'être*.

Mighty Moses heard the call from an Almighty God, and he moved a nation. We too are a people on the move, and as one of the group reminded me, we are running the race. We are forever setting our face and moving out because God is on the move behind us and ahead of us. As the session neared its end (and while there was still a little wine left in our glasses!), we stood as a group and remembered the words of Jesus, 'This is my blood which was shed for you.' The Passover story had moved on. Here was God's supreme saving act, here was God's Paschal Lamb, who with outstretched arms beckons and redeems the world.

When we drew to a close I hoped that we might all go home, that we might all go out, setting our face towards the challenges of life in the world, strengthened by our resolve, with a feeling of celebration in our hearts, secure and affirmed by God.

Touching on St Augustine

At another drop-in session I wondered what they would make of St Augustine. No sooner had I mentioned his name when one of the members questioned, light-heartedly, if we should be looking at him at all! Another member was quick to point out that Augustine's mother, Monica, prayed unceasingly

'Go back to your heart. Go back to God.'

for him. I felt there was something to work on here. This is the saint who said, 'Lord, change me—but not yet!' This caused a giggle. Augustine, I said, was a man of many desires and he lived life as if there were no tomorrow. But his insatiable appetite did not sustain him or feed him. One of his redeeming features was that he knew that he was not happy and that only a radical turnabout could bring him solace. He describes himself on one occasion as someone who had had 'a long wandering outside of himself.' 'Go back to yourself,' he cried, 'Go back to your heart. Go back to God.' It is not a bad place to start.

We read together an extract from one of his confessions. Then we read it again, and sat silently for a few minutes.

My heart is my whole being
It is the secret room that guards my identity
Where I am truly myself, where my life story unfolds
Outside of my heart I am lost
And there, in its silent depths
I can see the face of God
Whom I seek, for whom my heart is yearning.[7]

I wanted to provide a setting and the opportunity to put our thoughts into words so that we could hear our own voice and the voice of God. Using the words of St Augustine and with some additional poems, I began to create a mood of receptivity and attentiveness which so enables the theology of desire to come into play.

It had taken courage to speak about inner desires, hopes, loss, expectation—and mystery

I began by saying that most of us have been, at some time, where St Augustine has been, and that there was much to reflect on here. What does it mean to wander outside ourselves? When did we last lose touch with ourselves? When did we find ourselves? Where is God in all of this? What helps us to re-focus? What is our secret room? Do we guard our identity? We worked in pairs and those who wanted to share with the wider group did so. We shared harmony and disharmony and some experiences were too private to talk about. But we listened and some of us heard things about each other for the first time. It had taken courage to speak about inner desires, hopes, loss, expectation—and mystery. We spoke about our heartfelt experiences and encouraged each other to speak of their life story. We heard anecdotes, we listened to success and failure, to amazement and incredulity—in short we touched upon our spirituality. Some members of the group raised their own questions. 'Is anyone else still wandering like me?' 'Does mystery help or is it an easy way out?' 'Do we ever really know ourselves?' I hoped that from our discussions a sense of purpose would emerge, something we would want to share with others. What puzzles me sometimes about church life is our desire to keep spirituality for special occasions. Why do we highlight it one minute and put it away in a box the next? Spirituality does not come in a neat package which can be opened and aired. Nothing in our experience is ever complete because it moves on into thinking and being. If we believe that all our learning comes from God then it becomes a spiritual activity which breezes through everything giving us tremendous freedom to see the connectedness of things.

What puzzles me sometimes about church life is our desire to keep spirituality for special occasions

It had been a sad time for two members of the group as they had lost close friends. As chance would have it, I had with me one of the most beautiful of St Augustine's prayers.

> Blessed are those who love you O God, and love their friends in you and their enemies for your sake. They alone will never lose those who are dear to them, for they love them in one who is never lost.

In our closing prayers we thanked God for each other and for the gift of love and friendship. It was a time to be still and meet with God.

One of the younger women came up to me after the session and said, 'I didn't think it would be so spiritual.' I was not able to reply at the time and just smiled. However, when I arrived home I wanted to put into words what she was saying. I needed to clarify and reflect. It struck me that we should not be surprised if the spiritual is a surprise. It is good that it is because without surprise some of us would never get our feet off the ground. But it does not surprise God. If we believe that all our learning comes from God, then learning and theology becomes a spiritual activity which is perfectly normal and natural. Theology becomes part of our inner spirit that we hope to touch upon, and be strengthened by. I believe the excitement and expectancy of faith in our lives flows from this. This helps us to be a people

Theology becomes part of our inner spirit that we hope to touch upon, and be strengthened by

of mission because our theology is personal, passionate and earthed in our humanity. However, not everything goes to plan. Sometimes discussion dries up and I am left stuck for words, feeling inept. Again, not everyone takes to my pictures. All I can do is to allow time for the disappointment to subside and then pick myself up again.

This helps us to be a people of mission because our theology is personal, passionate and earthed in our humanity

The Dancing Christ

A picture of the *Dancing Christ* by Bagong Kussudiaraja brought its own surprise and risk to one of my groups.[8] It shows Jesus dancing (ascending) his way to heaven. It was new to everyone. Not only did I want to share with them the excitement of the *Dancing Christ*, I also wanted to finish with a joyous dance of the risen Lord where our hearts and minds and bodies were taken up into one. But would they dance with me?

I realized that I would have to ease my way in. We began by looking at the picture. The agony is behind Jesus and now there is unspeakable joy. We spent some time reflecting upon these words by Anthony de Mello who directs our gaze to the *Dancing Christ* so that we can see more.

> God 'dances' creation. God is the dancer. Creation is his dance. The dance is different from the dancer, yet it has no existence apart from him. You cannot take it home in a box. The moment the dancer stops the dance ceases to be…Be silent, and contemplate the Dance. Just look. A star, a flower, a fading leaf, a bird, a stone, any fragment of the Dance will do. And hopefully it won't be long before you see the Dancer![9]

Spread out on a nearby table were pictures, postcards and posters depicting a variety of 'movement.' Pictures of arches, pillars, bridges, cats, dancers, the joy of a child clapping and flowers—anything I could lay my hand on. I asked them to choose very carefully two pictures which 'stop you in your tracks' and then to say why it had had this effect. They were to sit quietly for five minutes with the pictures and then I asked them to share their thoughts with another person and, if they so wished, with everyone. This took time. Indeed it was necessary to allow time for the movement to take hold. We shared our thoughts which were so unbelievably diverse, and then we traced some of the movements in the air—tall pillars, graceful arches, sweeping bridges, sinewy cats, the stretch of a dancer at the moment of perfection, and spiky flower heads.

We stood in a space. I gave the lead and using these movements we danced a dance of joy to the pulsating beat of Floyd Kramer's 'On the Rebound.' We held our final movement and then to my surprise and delight spontaneous applause broke out. We were part of God's dance. We stretched up and reached out with the risen Dancing Christ. We were part of that unspeakable joy, here, today.

Questions for Reflection

1. When has theology helped to make sense of your life as you see it?
2. 'Theology thrills us and drills us'—Does it? In what ways have you experienced this and in what ways has it failed to do so?
3. 'Theology, like the attentive lover, won't leave us alone' How far can you agree with that from your experience?
4. If theology is a 'spiritual quest' what does it mean to live and move and have our being in God? Reflect on the occasion when theology has not felt like this.
5. If God is a 'God of temptation' and a 'God of desire' can one prepare for such an experience? What do you say?
6. When does your faith dance?

Risking Your Life with Theology 4

'To live is to change,' said Cardinal Newman.

It sounds simple, just like breathing. But is it? Change is something most of us take for granted. One look in the mirror tells its own story, though some of us may rebel. Living too is something that is and experience tells us that no matter what happens to us we simply have to get on with living.

It has been said that 'the unexamined life is not worth living.' However, Socrates' words can only be understood when we come to realize what we might have missed. We do not miss that of which we are unaware. Here is where a theology of desire can come into its own, because it bids us, draws us to examine and re-examine our lives. It requires that we pause to reflect in order to take stock of ourselves in God's world. It is a kind of repentance which not only demands conscious effort but which may require help. Change is synonymous with a theology of desire, and is a much more self conscious development, and needs to be if we are to be fulfilled as God's people. A neat definition of learning has been expressed as an enduring change brought about by experience. It is the word enduring that matters, for in order for our learning and our theology to be sustained, understood and taken on board, all of us from time to time need help. Experience is not enough. We may well miss the meaning. We need help to change, to get through life and, if we accept the need for help and the need to learn, then our theology prepares us for a changing life.

earning has been expressed as an enduring change brought about by experience

Those of us who are involved in helping others to learn need to bring to consciousness, with care, the risk factor in doing theology. We need to bring a sense of urgency to it all. Whilst knowing what we need to know as a Christian is beneficial, knowing that we have the freedom to interpret what we know is even more important. The interpretation of life in the light of faith, which is part of the risk factor, can be excluded or worse still tagged on at the end of our thinking.

Doing theology, in my experience, is often haphazard in the churches and in order to fill the gaps, courses are written and sometimes seized upon by clergy and lay people alike. But here there is the danger of failing to take a critical look at the theology behind the words, and at the way of doing theology. Our gaze is so often turned inward, and, believed to be spiritual, ends up cosy and constraining. This type of theology makes us visible in the church but invisible in the world and so we may well find our niche in church structures but not in the world.

This type of theology makes us visible in the church but invisible in the world

I cannot ignore at this stage, the *Alpha* course which is being presented in many churches up and down the country. *Alpha* wears its heart on its sleeve for God. Where else in the Church of England is God's invitation so boldly announced to an aching world? I commend *Alpha* for its feast and fellowship. I am a supporter as well as a critic. I am keen to give my support to its evangelistic outreach as long as it is allied to critical thought. However, *Alpha* has tended to shy away from criticism. *Alpha*, it seems, owns *Alpha*. But as you know, any book or course that is let loose in the world has just taken the biggest risk imaginable. It is out there, it is free to be looked at, criticized, read, adapted, updated, gobbled up or spat out.

Theology becomes part of our longing and yearning in the heart of God. We are free to experience new ways of thinking and new ways of interpreting. And this, all this, by the grace of God. Situations arise and there are no neat conclusions. Questions seem to raise more questions, and so we need to have a willingness to grapple with issues knowing that God is in it all. Learning to take theology seriously is something that many of us have not faced up to in our churches. The whole nature of what it means to learn is rarely discussed openly, mainly because when it comes to learning and doing theology we are a people of timidity, lay and clergy alike, a little spoon fed, and either we have not the courage or have not been encouraged to take (sacrificial?) risks. By this I mean a conscious willingness, a conscious desire to become part of the language of education and theology and to engage in life changing and risk taking experiences which require further exploration. The feel-good factor has surely had its day because we cannot go on believing everything in the garden is rosy, either in ourselves or in our churches, when we feel in our bones it is not. Risk is at the heart of Christian learning and encounter. It is at the very heart of doing theology. This is part of God's way of teaching us and calling us to obedience.

Risk is at the heart of Christian learning and encounter

A Working Theology for All

What we need is an everyday working theology for all, which will test our sense of vocation and which is backed up by a theological education that supports and feeds our desires and stimulates our thinking in our daily lives, and in our worldly lives. We need to be equipped with a faith that has everything to do with the world. A faith which is learned and then lived out only in the confines of our church lives, shrivels. I am not saying anything new, but why are the churches so reluctant to put theology and education for all at the top of their agenda?

We have a tremendous public relations job to do in our churches if we want theology and education to become centre stage. If we are required to think diligently and clearly about what we are doing then we need to speak in more positive ways about the whole nature of theology and education. Whilst education *is not everything*, like theology *it is in everything*, inspiring us, sustaining us and creating in us vision and hope. So why are we dragging our feet? Why do we not believe that theological education can do great things for the people of God? And why are we not more aware that when we put 'Christian' in front of 'education' that together they have the power to transform? Together they have bite. Similarly when education and theology are brought together, our thinking is sharpened, our expectations are raised, because we seek and see new depths inside and outside of ourselves.

Why do we not believe that theological education can do great things for the people of God?

Sadly the word education which of its essence means to draw-out-and-lead-on captivates only a minority in our churches. And yet this leading-out-into, this calling out, is essential for all of us who are trying to discern our vocation and how to use our God-given gifts. With a little imagination we can see that it is a sign of the kingdom breaking into our lives which draws upon our inventiveness and our personhood. It is doing theology at its best.

We have a battle on our hands. The question is how do we safeguard education in our churches so we remain focussed on its true meaning and value? And if a theologically educated laity is a liberating force, why are we not taking advantage of it by freeing our imagination and finding our voice?

One of the problems for not taking theology seriously is that the church is wanting to put more of its eggs into one basket, that is, into lay training. I am all for lay training and have vigorously supported shared ministry and lay participation, but not at the expense and neglect of doing theology. First and foremost we need a theologically educated laity. Training, as distinct from theological education, is about fostering, deepening and owning the skills we have and using them with others. We are helped by those with relevant expertise to set up structures for those who have heard God's call to become part of God's work through lay ministry in the church and for the world. This may be for mission, evangelism, teaching, pastoral work or whatever the need is seen to be. Whilst a great deal of this is still in the theoretical stage for some parishes, the overall aim is to use lay gifts so that we can work alongside the clergy. This is quite laudable, but as a result lay theological education can so easily become the Cinderella, brushed to one side and hidden away in the corner.

In actual fact many of us who come to our churches do not want to train for anything. We have usually done our training for our life's work and may even have to train again. Most of us are in training already in that we are bringing up our families, coping with married life and aged parents, or we are holding down a job and exploring hobbies and leisure interests. Whilst there are some of us who wish to present ourselves for lay training, the vast majority of us are going the other way, or should be, out into the world learning to risk our lives for God.

Teaching and Learning

5

Keeping Your Nerve

So theology unnerves us and education scares us. Well I have to admit that I also feel a little wary when I read these words from James 3.1: 'You know that we teachers shall be judged more severely than other men.' James appears to discourage many of his readers from becoming teachers because of the high responsibility demanded of them. The risks are enormous. To enter the teaching profession is, like marriage, not to be taken lightly. It seems to me that we may well be in danger of taking teaching too lightly in the church today, and if this is so then we are in trouble. But is it so obvious?

Clergy nowadays simply find themselves in the teaching role; it is part of their job, and they have no choice. But what of the risks? I do not actually believe that the church as a body has examined these risks, not because it is frightened by them but because *it does not see the need to.* And why is talk of the teacher and the role of the teacher unfashionable and at times distasteful in the church today? I do not find it at all helpful when people say, 'We don't teach; we enable others to learn.'[10] Surely the line is too finely drawn. You do not teach if you cannot enable. You cannot enable and not teach. What we forget is that teaching is all about *how* we enable and facilitate, and these activities draw heavily upon the teacher as a *person*. What surprises me is the attack on such a noble word. And yet we preach lifelong learning.

Why is talk of the teacher unfashionable and at times distasteful in the church today?

I believe we have belittled and dishonoured the role of the teacher in the church today, and have put very little in its place. What also upsets me is the patronizing view that teaching is really about imparting knowledge and information to the ignorant, in an authoritarian and didactic manner.

I have met clergy who are wary of their teaching role and of their own teaching ability. I share in their wariness. What we really need to recognize is that teaching, at its best, probes into our thinking patterns, clearing the way and helping to clarify thought. It helps to sharpen our awareness by encouraging us to find perspective and meaning in our lives. It enables and deepens our experience. Without this unclouding process we are in danger of remaining hidden, not only from ourselves, but from each other. Worse still we may succeed in stifling each other. I have no doubt that the church, in theory, believes the heart of teaching to be about learning, changing and growing. But in practise when it comes to exploring and implementing these far reaching words, it buckles at the knees. Why?

A Lack of Awareness

A lot of this has to do with a lack of awareness about what it means to have an educated laity and how to teach them. We pay lip service to the notion of an educated laity whilst recognizing, unreservedly, the need for an educated clergy. We have taken learning seriously for the clergy at the expense of the laity. We have failed to identify, appreciate and develop the role of the teacher within the clergy role, because we have not attached the importance of this role to life long learning for lay people in the church.

With all this in mind I feel I am bound to ask this question which has been haunting me for some years—*does the church really want teachers?* Undoubtedly it will say yes, but why does it not support its clergy and lay teachers to become better teachers? Why does it not provide money for on-going systematic training for improving teaching ability? Why does it not believe that this can make a difference? Half a dozen lectures for ordinands at theological college on theological education for the laity will not do. If the theological colleges pay scant attention to the teaching skills of their students then it can follow that the churches in turn pay scant attention to the teaching of the laity. If theology does not combine with education then the theology which is going on all the time in the parishes may remain hidden, shallow and dry. Is it not the role of the lay teacher and the priest-as-teacher to put new life into dry bones? Many of our newly ordained need help on the shop floor in their local churches where they soon find out that doing theology with the laity is full of risk, because they do not give you too many chances! I dare say this because I have met with clergy who admit to not being good teachers, and I have also met young curates who feel lacking because they know too little about how to teach.

Only then can we go on to say how we should inspire, encourage and train clergy and laity to become better teachers

We need to go back to basics and we should begin by asking these questions: What *is* a teacher? What is a teacher *for*? and *Why* do we need teachers? Only then, I believe, can we go on to say how we should inspire, encourage and train clergy and laity to become better teachers. And we do this best by drawing upon, and awakening, the God-given imagination of all those who, by their calling, find themselves in the role of teacher.

The church needs to give dignity back to the teacher. But more than this is required. We need to dig deep into our reserves and discover 'the education of desire,' that is, we need to 'desire better, to desire more, and above all, to desire in a different way.'[11] This is the language of risk which is part of the teacher's language. It is also the language of hope which is awesomely discovered in our theological quest.

The Teacher as a Person

The theologian and educationalist Martin Buber has come to my attention late in life. How I wish I had met him earlier. I think he gives dignity back to the teacher as a person. If you have ever doubted who you are then dip into Buber and feel alive again. Whilst he restored my confidence as a teacher doing theology, I think he has something to say to all of us because he describes just what the church is missing. Again his understanding of the teacher is a healthy corrective to a fashionable and depressingly negative interpretation.

He reminds us that there was a time 'when there neither was, nor needed to be, any specific calling of educator or teacher. Yet teaching took place. There was instead, a master, a philosopher or a coppersmith, whose journeymen and apprentices lived with him, and learned by being allowed to share in what he had to teach them of his handicraft or brainwork. These persons learned without noticing that they did, the mystery of personal life: they received the spirit.'[12] As you can see there is more to this than just learning skills. Can it be described as catching the 'spark of life,' or being swept up by 'a theology of desire,' and of sharing that which is held sacred, holy and precious? Is it a meeting of our need, as the Augustinian nuns say, for 'someone to whom we can relate with our human experience...who shows us the way to find our true selves...who goes before us in the stupendous and arduous ways of God'?[13] If so, then this sort of learning, and I would add, this way of doing theology, can mean a never ending discovery of meeting with oneself through, and in, the joy of meeting others.

This sort of learning can mean a never ending discovery of meeting with oneself through, and in, the joy of meeting others

The master, as you can see, remains a proper model for the teacher. However—and this is crucial—on this model the educator, if he has to act consciously, must do it *'as though he did not.'* According to Buber there is 'influence but there must be no hint of interference. The educator finds himself/herself in the midst of need by being a bit deeper in it, in the midst of service by being a little higher up, but it is a status which he invokes *without words.'*[14] What is important to grasp here is that Buber directs our thinking to the majesty and mystery surrounding the teacher and pupil, and it is precisely at this point that the teacher as a person is valued. As teachers, unless we have pondered the mystery of our own being, we are unlikely to convey 'a fragment of that mystery which surrounds all being.'[15] Remember the doctors of the law were astounded at Jesus' teaching, because he taught with authority. But Jesus' authority was personal and needed no authorization and so was self authenticating because it was always an answer, an answer to questions his pupils raised and which he by his *person*, provoked.[16] Thus could Jesus the master, the model, act and teach as though he did not. He influenced but did not interfere. He invoked without words his servant role, which paradoxically became that of master-teacher.

Remember the doctors of the law were astounded at Jesus' teaching, because he taught with authority

Let us put the teacher as a person back into education. Let us learn to do theology in such a natural way that the teacher is not seen as a threat but rather as a person who with precious hands draws others out and leads them on unobtrusively. Perhaps we have to go on discovering that teaching is an art, that life is an art, and that theology is a living well, so that when we come to learn together, our learning and our living is lived out in creative ways. What is important here is how we see each other, how we behave with each other, and how we talk with each other. And this may depend on how we risk our lives doing theology and the value we place on education.

Questions for Reflection

1 'Risking your life with theology'—where and when does the risk factor come to bear on your faith journey?

2 'Theology scares us and education unnerves us' what is your experience? How can you help others who think like this?

3 'I'm not spiritual enough!' 'I'm not good enough!' In what ways can you restore self-worth in a person?

4 What is needed to make theology come alive for you and for your church?

Notes

1 E Templeton, personal communication.

2 A Dyson, 'Clericalism, Church and Laity,' in *All Are Called: Towards a Theology of the Laity* (London: Church Information Office / General Synod Board of Education Report, 1985).

3 E Peterson, *Under the Unpredictable Plant: An exploration in Vocational Holiness* (Grand Rapids, Michigan: Eerdmans, 1992).

4 E Farley, *Theologia; The Fragmentation and Unity of Theological Education* (Philadelphia: Fortress Press, 1983).

5 *The Five Marks of Mission* (The United Society for the Propagation of the Gospel).

6 H Walton, 'An Abuse of Power 2: A Polemic Concerning the Priests of God and the Ministers of Religion,' in *Modern Churchman*, New Series, Vol XXXIV, No 2, 1992.

7 M Guerrini, OSA, *Late Have I Loved You* (Slough: St Paul Publications, 1986).

8 B Kussudiardja, 'The Ascension of Jesus,' in M Takemaka and R O'Grady (eds), *The Bible Through Asian Eyes* (New Zealand: Pace Publishing in association with Asian Christian Art, 1991).

9 Anthony de Mello in *The Bible Through Asian Eyes.*

10 D Goodbourn, 'Theological Training for Christian Education,' in *Education in Church Today,* No 5, Summer, 1991.

11 E P Thompson, *William Morris: Romantic to Revolutionary* (London: Merlin, 1977). Quoted by Peter Jarvis in, P Jarvis and N Walters (eds), *Adult Education and Theological Interpretations* (Malabar, Fla: Krieger, 1993).

12 M Buber, 'Education,' in *Between Man and Man* (trans R G Smith, London: Kegan Paul, 1947).

13 M Guerrini, OSA, *Late Have I Loved You.*

14 M Buber, 'Education,' in *Between Man and Man.*

15 D Webster, 'A Spiritual Dimension for Education,' *Theology*, 88, 721, Jan 1985.

16 Prebendary D C Ford, 'The Teacher's Ultimate Authority,' in E Hulmes and B Watson (eds), *Religious Studies and Public Examinations* (Oxford: Farmington Institute for Christian Studies, 1980).